ZENDAYA

FAMOUS ENTERTAINER

Big Buddy Books
An Imprint of Abdo Publishing
abdopublishing.com

BIG BUDDY POP BIOGRAPHIES

KATIE LAJINESS

abdopublishing.com

Published by Abdo Publishing, a division of ABDO, PO Box 398166, Minneapolis, Minnesota 55439.
Copyright © 2018 by Abdo Consulting Group, Inc. International copyrights reserved in all countries.
No part of this book may be reproduced in any form without written permission from the publisher.
Big Buddy Books™ is a trademark and logo of Abdo Publishing.

Printed in the United States of America, North Mankato, Minnesota.
092017
012018

THIS BOOK CONTAINS
RECYCLED MATERIALS

Cover Photo: Angela Weiss/Getty Images.
Interior Photos: Alberto E. Rodriguez/Getty Images (pp. 17, 27); Craig Barritt/Getty Images (p. 25);
    Dimitrios Kambouris/Getty Images (pp. 5, 21); Earl Gibson III/Getty Images (p. 6); Frazer Harrison/
    Getty Images (p. 23); Kevork Djansezian/Getty Images (p. 19); Kevin Winter/Getty Images
    (p. 29); Michael Buckner/Getty Images (p. 13); Rob Carr/Getty Images (p. 15); Valerie Macon/
    Getty Images (p. 9); ZUMA Press, Inc./Alamy Stock Photo (p. 11).

Coordinating Series Editor: Tamara L. Britton
Contributing Editor: Jill Roesler
Graphic Design: Jenny Christensen

Publisher's Cataloging-in-Publication Data

Names: Lajiness, Katie, author.
Title: Zendaya / by Katie Lajiness.
Description: Minneapolis, Minnesota : Abdo Publishing, 2018. | Series: Big buddy pop biographies |
    Includes online resources and index.
Identifiers: LCCN 2017943904 | ISBN 9781532112201 (lib.bdg.) | ISBN 9781614799276 (ebook)
Subjects: LCSH: Zendaya (Zendaya Coleman), 1996-.--Juvenile literature. | Singers--Juvenile literature. |
    Actors--Juvenile literature. | United States--Juvenile literature.
Classification: DDC 782.42164092 [B]--dc23
LC record available at https://lccn.loc.gov/2017943904

CONTENTS

A BRIGHT STAR

Zendaya is a talented **performer**. She was first known as the star of *Shake It Up!* Today, Zendaya is an actress, singer, dancer, and model. She is also making a name for herself as a businesswoman. Fans love to chat about Zendaya on **social media**.

DID YOU KNOW ?
Zendaya's name is pronounced zehn-DAY-uh.

SNAPSHOT

NAME:
Zendaya Maree
Stoermer Coleman

BIRTHDAY:
September 1, 1996

BIRTHPLACE:
Oakland, California

TELEVISION SHOWS:
Shake It Up!, K.C. Undercover

FAMILY TIES

Zendaya Maree Stoermer Coleman was born in Oakland, California, on September 1, 1996. Her parents are Claire Stoermer and Kazembe Ajamu Coleman. She has three sisters and two brothers.

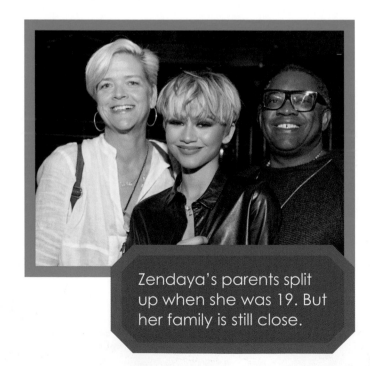

Zendaya's parents split up when she was 19. But her family is still close.

DID YOU KNOW
Zendaya has nieces and nephews older than she is!

WHERE IN THE WORLD?

Oregon

Idaho

Nevada

Utah

Oakland

California

Arizona

PACIFIC OCEAN

EARLY YEARS

Early on, Zendaya found success as an actress and dancer. In 2006, she was in a summer program at the California Shakespeare Theater.

Zendaya also loved to dance. She was a member of a **hip-hop** group. Zendaya also studied hula dancing at the Academy of Hawaiian Arts.

Growing up, Zendaya spent a lot of time in the theater. Her mother was a stage manager.

SHAKE IT UP!

When Zendaya was 14, she won a **role** in the Disney series *Shake It Up!* She played a character named Rocky Blue. The part showed off her dancing and acting skills.

DID YOU KNOW?

For this role, Zendaya and her dad moved to Los Angeles, California.

Zendaya and actress Bella Thorne played skilled dancers who perform on a local TV show.

On set, life was busy for Zendaya. The cast filmed a new **episode** every week. Between scenes, she worked with a **tutor**. After a long day of shooting, Zendaya did **promotional** events to support the show.

DID YOU KNOW ?

Shake It Up! was on the air for three seasons.

Off the set, Zendaya (*left*) spent time with Disney stars Debby Ryan (*center*) and Bella Thorne (*right*).

BIG VOICE

Zendaya has a big singing voice. In 2012, she signed a record deal. At 17, Zendaya **released** her self-titled album. Her single "Replay" reached number 40 on the *Billboard* **Pop** Digital Songs chart.

"Replay" sold more than 1 million copies! It has been watched more than 154 million times on the website YouTube.

K.C. UNDERCOVER

In 2014, Zendaya won another lead **role**. In the Disney series *K.C. Undercover*, she plays a student who learns that her parents are **spies**. The show lasted two seasons.

DID YOU KNOW ?

In 2016, Zendaya released the song "Something New" with singer Chris Brown.

Zendaya won big at the 2016 Nickelodeon Kids' Choice Awards. She took home the Favorite Female TV Star award for *K.C. Undercover*.

BUSINESSWOMAN

Zendaya is much more than a **performer**. She is also a smart businesswoman. As a successful **designer**, she created a clothing line called Daya by Zendaya. She even has her own **app**. It gives fans access to her videos, music, and products.

Zendaya wrote a book called *Between U and Me: How to Rock Your Tween Years with Style and Confidence.*

MEDIA DARLING

Zendaya had become a superstar. She was very popular on **social media**. As of 2017, she had more than 41 million followers on Instagram. And, more than 7 million people followed her on Twitter.

DID YOU KNOW?
Zendaya was a model for COVERGIRL makeup.

Zendaya took time to pose with her fans. The fans would often post the photos on social media.

Zendaya often appeared in the **media**. She has been featured on magazine covers. She has also been a guest on *The Ellen DeGeneres Show*.

Although she kept busy, Zendaya took time to help her famous friends. She played a superhero in Taylor Swift's "Bad Blood" music video.

Zendaya (*right*) joined *Project Runway* as a guest judge in September 2016.

GIVING BACK

Zendaya enjoys giving back to help struggling people. She spent her eighteenth birthday raising money for feedONE. This group helps feed children in poor countries around the world. Two years later, Zendaya raised $50,000 to help poor women start businesses.

In 2014, Zendaya visited a school in New York City, New York, as part of a group called UNICEF.

DANCING WITH THE STARS

In 2013, Zendaya was on Season 16 of *Dancing With the Stars*. On the show, a famous person is paired with a **professional** dancer. Couples **compete** to win a special **trophy**. The public can vote for their favorite couple. Zendaya and her partner won second place!

DID YOU KNOW ?
Zendaya performed dances such as the tango and hip-hop.

On the show, Zendaya partnered with professional dancer Valentin Chmerkovskiy.

BUZZ

In 2017, Zendaya had a busy year. She starred in the movies *The Greatest Showman* and *Spider-Man: Homecoming.*

She worked with singer Prince Royce on the song "X" for his new album. Fans are excited to see what Zendaya does next!

Zendaya won Favorite TV Actress at the 2017 Kids' Choice Awards.

GLOSSARY

app a computer program that performs a special function.

compete to take part in a contest between two or more persons or groups.

designer (dih-ZINE-uhr) someone who has ideas and works on making a plan.

episode one show in a series of shows.

hip-hop a form of popular music that features rhyme, spoken words, and electronic sounds. It is similar to rap music.

media ways of sharing information, especially with large groups of people. Radio, television, newspapers, and magazines are examples of media.

performer someone who performs.

pop relating to popular music.

professional (pruh-FEHSH-nuhl) a person who works for money rather than only for pleasure.

promotional aimed at helping something become known.

release to make available to the public.

role a part an actor plays.

social media a form of communication on the Internet where people can share information, messages, and videos. It may include blogs and online groups.

spy one who secretly watches what others are doing.

trophy (TROH-fee) an award for success.

tutor (TOO-tuhr) someone who teaches a student privately.

ONLINE RESOURCES

Booklinks
NONFICTION NETWORK
FREE! ONLINE NONFICTION RESOURCES

To learn more about Zendaya, visit **abdobooklinks.com**.
These links are routinely monitored and updated to provide
the most current information available.

INDEX